Men Get Divorced

Truths from the Hearts, Souls & Minds of Divorced Men

By

Paul Stanley

For my loving parents, my beautiful children…

…*and* your beautiful children

Edited by: Aleatha Hoff

Cover Design by: John Droese

ISBN: 978-0-6151-6450-2

WHY MEN GET DIVORCED

Foreword

Author Stanley noted that in addition to his own divorce, that way too many of his friends were also divorced or divorcing. When he looked from the outside in and through his friends' eyes and ordeals, he strangely noticed an almost "invisible" communication gap between spouses and ex-spouses, atypical to the usual well documented male, female communication "problems."

This "invisible" truth he primarily attributed to men but to women as well when it came to truly understanding or even knowing the real "truths" of men.

Most importantly, sadly he noted what all of this is doing to our children before, during or after a divorce and the continuing toll it takes on them no matter how much denial the spouses or ex-spouses may be in.

The "invisible" became visible when many, many men started sharing their "secrets, confusion and pain" with him in addition to his own experience. Paul simply couldn't find any book that dealt with these real truths. So, he wrote it. Men Get Divorced: Truths from the Hearts, Souls and Minds of Divorced Men is finally a book that reveals and sets into words these truths, secrets, fears and emotions of men. As one divorced female friend said to him, "finally, now I get it, why didn't you write it years ago? It actually may have made a difference back then."

Stanley knew he was on to something when he let a close friend who was teetering on divorce read the manuscript. His friend couldn't get over how he so related to almost every page. How it "spoke" to and "for" him actually giving him comfort and the ability to better get through his ordeal.

Another friend begged Paul to send the manuscript to his estranged wife. It actually opened up the lines of communication between them that is so sorely missing in relationships today.

This may be one answer as to why.

Introduction

Divorce – it's a horrible gut wrenching, mind numbing voyage into a dark and uncharted sea. And whether you're the one tossed overboard, or the mutineer; whether a storm is always brewing in your collective lives or you're riding the waves of one that passed. It's one of the most sea-sickening, nauseating voyages you can take in your life, as well as for the passengers in your life too.

Then why are we all doing it? Why are we all abandoning ship? Why? What makes us run instead of standing and fighting for our marriage? What sinks us and our vowed ocean of love into a sea of Muck and Meier?

You stood next to me and we both took a vow. Now you stand near me separated by a lawyer. A stranger in a strange place, where strangers tell us we are no longer as one. A surreal view as shadowy figures claw and pick through the ashes of what was our sacred phoenix of love, hopes, dreams, family and nest eggs.

And why is it so easy to break up a union and shatter the lives we so cherished? Why has it become the norm? We all suffer, we all wonder, and we are all not alone in our quiet desperation – we just don't know that.

Men, especially men, seldom let on. After all, we're men taught through years of conditioning and past "voices" we must be men – men don't cry, men don't feel, men move on. In reality, we share the same burning desire to know. We yearn for our questions to be answered.

And, we hurt. We hurt badly. We're also scared to death.

I'm not a PhD or a researcher. I'm merely a man. A divorced man and a man other men opened up to. I don't profess that this book will bring relief to either side. But it may shed some light. It may answer some of those questions we never know or are afraid once again to ask.

It will speak the truth as I know it, as a man whose "been there and done that" in addition to the truths shared with me by other men; I simply put these emotions, fears and thoughts into words.

If this brings you some form of comfort, if it answers some questions or simply makes you think, then that's a good thing – because we are not all alone in our "quiet desperation." We are all simply desperate to know and so afraid to ask.

So, if these truths and insights help us all learn to avoid misery, before, during or after a divorce or to not repeat our mistakes, maybe all of us will finally be better off. I know the children will. And we simply cannot continue to do this to our children. We just can't. They are our most precious of all life's beauties and yet they don't even have a moments say. We big adults make decisions that can be so detrimental to their very being.

If this helps you help them, whatever stage you're in, what could be better?

What about you? Do you really think you simply just change a member of your family and life remains as it always has? Not much else changes; your "status," your finances? That couldn't be further from the truth.

If you're contemplating divorce and these simple pages can make you stop and think even for one more precious second, a second that leads you into thoughts you never even contemplated. Leads you to "fight" for what you once cherished and valued so dear to defend and rescue all the lives that will ripple.

Or, to simply get along after the divorce, for everyone's well being, and again, especially for the children, then that's a real good thing too.

Remember, you can always get a divorce, but you can't get a true love that was worth fighting for, a family that is everything to fight for; if you don't fight, if you don't know, if you don't understand. And, apparently we don't and shame on us. You'll never understand pre or post marriage if you simply don't share the truth and communicate and try and understand each other and ourselves.

And what about post divorce life? Did you know that second marriage failure rates are around 85%! Obviously, we haven't learned. So, if this helps us all to do it "right" the next time around, again, we have to do something.

Either way, in or out, pre or post, male or female, there's everything to gain or everything to lose. It has always been your choice maybe just not an enlightened one.

And, I believe there is this "invisible" communication gap between men and women that hopefully the book can help close before, during or after a divorce.

And, one other very important thing we all need to see and finally see through-- the lawyers. Funny how we didn't need them to get married, but here they are during our most vulnerable time. One that is easily manipulated, and boy do they ever! Because of course it's a time of money. It's time to wake up to the pillage and havoc these people wreck; especially since it's beyond critical that you remain friends with your ex and you hang on to all of the finances that you can. You're going to need both. Know that both of you can still do this between only the two of you.

I'm only here to tell the truth as a man, and to let other men know it is ok to feel what you feel, think what you think and to let women know that we do feel and what we feel, what we think, what we fear.

Women wear it on their sleeves, we men roll ours up. That doesn't seem to be working for us does it? So here are some truths from the hearts, souls and minds of divorced men. And maybe just maybe, we can bridge this ever widening abyss and shine a much needed light on what in truth we men are wrestling with as we wrestle with you and our lives as men.

So it begins.

Today I mourned my marriage. Today I buried my one time best friend.

Today I felt a sadness known so few times to me but so powerful, it doomed me and us, from the start.

We can only change the things we can change, and even my pleas and promises can't change this.

Can I change the past through my future actions?

I won't be given the chance to even try. Not in this relationship anyway.

So where do we go from here? They say there's life after death.

But any life without you is half a life at best.

And so how do I make it whole.

Today I mourned my marriage. Today my soul ached for my one time mate.

Why did it now become so clear? Why did I ignore it all? Why did I do it all?

Why couldn't you help me see? Did I constantly test you?

Did I subconsciously want to test the boundaries of your love for me?

Did I need you to prove you would never leave?

Why did fear once again rule my life, and when is it ever going to stop?

I see it now, why not then?

I can be the person I want to be, the one you knew I could be, the one we both wanted me to be, but I was afraid to show you… and me.

Would he want you to know that today he buried his one time best friend and not only mourned a marriage, but mourned what could have been?

In the end the man she knew he was and waited for with her last ounce of strength, in some perverse way, finally appeared and took his revenge on her behalf. For today he buried his one time best friend, along with the man that slew her love.

So where do we go from here?

Today I am so sad. It took you great courage, I know.

The assumptions of your anger, they bind and hold. They push and sting.

They play havoc with my present moment.

It's said that one path to a happier life is to stop making assumptions.

But isn't that all we've been taught?

And are not we trained to assume an outcome our heart or mind only wishes or fears?

Ask question for the answers negate the assumptions.

But I can't ask you. For your anger's origin is only my assumption.

And whatever it is, it simply won't let me near and certainly won't let me in.

So what would I ask you or say to you if you'd let me or I'd let me?

Do you think of me? Do you forgive me, I'll forgive you.

Does our horrible past together seem less horrible now?

What about the anger and what makes you think any of it will be any better?

Denial, anger, resolution or buyers remorse-where are you at?

If you're internal judge stepped down from the bench for even a moment.

What else would I not be afraid to ask?

My assumption is that your anger contains a love and a fear of a love for me. So my question is… does it?

Anger usually goes hand in hand with fear. My assumption is that you fear having or admitting any attachment to me whatsoever.

Do you?

Or heaven forbid maybe having made a mistake.

Did you?

My assumption is there would be a way back for us if I could show you, hold you, take you by the hand – and assure you, but it isn't so, is it?

I assume I would look silly presenting any of this to you. Would I?

Is there even the smallest, faintest voice within you that even remotely hopes I would?

Or have you silenced and gagged it – forever?

I assume you have… am I right?

I hurt!

Why won't you help me? It's me! This is me! Remember?
You would never sit there and watch me hurt like this? Remember?
It's still me.

I may be caged with every bar I ripped from your ribs that finally exposed and damaged your heart.
The light above my cage has also dimmed, I know.
Your fear is a stronger lock than anything man made.

But I know I hurt. Why won't you help me? It's me! Remember?
It's me.

I know, I could never admit that before. It's just how we are.
But we do hope you notice.
Not that we'd ever admit that.

I'm looking at a mountain – and I seem so small.

Our problems seem but a grain of sand.

Because I'm looking at a mountain and one that I couldn't begin to climb.

I wonder… if you saw this mountain, would my trespasses seem so grand?

Would you take my hand and say we can step over them together if you saw this mountain?

It's been here forever.

We were a fleeting second.

Then why couldn't we climb our molehill?

I wish you could see this mountain.

I'm watching two ducks. They're so beautiful. Preening, each other.

Did you know ducks mate for life?

They raise their kids together.

Did you know that if one mate dies, the other will not leave its side? It'll lay over it to protect it. Even in a storm, a really bad storm.

They stay together in life and death. So not even till death do they part.

Like you said…

And yet they're just ducks.

Why are you so angry?

See, that's what throws me.

If you really don't love me anymore, if you really don't give a damn, why are you so angry?

I was told that a person is not ready for a divorce until they can walk away with no emotions.

No emotions at all.

Anger is a big one. And what the hell are you so angry about?

This was your divorce. I would think you'd be happy.

Oh, I know, you are happy. You've told me that many times.

But why are you so angry?

If I wasn't such a jerk, you wouldn't be in this position? That's just a guess.

The divorce didn't go the way you thought it would?

How is something so vile, so disruptive supposed to go?

If only I had... you fill in the blank.

Because I don't know what else I could have done.

Why are you so angry?

Yes, I'd really like to know.

You confuse me… and during a very confusing time to begin with.

You say one thing, yet, at this time, you do another. So you leave me wondering. Do actions speak louder than words? And your words are as loud as they get?

So which is it?

Why do you scream one thing and do another or is that my imagination again too as you would say.

See what I mean? You confuse me.

I so wish you would just talk to me. Like we use to.

Or not even like we use to; just honest though.

We might as well practice now.

Because, like it or not, we will need to talk. Truly communicate for many years to come. That is if you expect our children to have a decent chance at all.

So will you just try and talk with me? Not at me.

If part of your fear in so doing is that you're really not one hundred percent sure. Then just tell me that. Will you?

I won't use it as false hope. I promise.

After all, we have come so far apart. Why mess that up, huh? And I also won't use it against you, should the inevitable occur. Are you afraid that by telling me some hidden truths you may be telling yourself at the same time? And if that becomes the case, what is the real harm? You seem to be on a course that you are either not sure of at times, or need to stick with at all costs for whatever reasons.

So is it merely a slip when you're momentarily nice, your conscience?

A flicker of love?

A fear of all of the above?

Or none of the above?

So yes, I'm confused. And maybe it's because you are too. Are you? Tell me. Think about it. Talk with me. Even if you think you can't.

Why can't I hear you when you tell me you don't love me anymore? Why don't I believe you when you tell me we're through? It's over or so you say…

It's that look in your eyes. That momentary pull back when we see each other.

Is it projection? Assumption? Denial?

I don't know. But something's there, at least I think there is.

Maybe I don't want to hear you. Maybe I don't want to believe you. Sure, that's part of it. But I know you! That, a judge can't take away.

And I'm sure I don't want to believe you or hear you in the first place.

Yes, I may be afraid to.

But I also need you to make me believe, to hear.

If you're really not coming back, I really do need to believe.

Of course you couldn't make me hear the problems nor believe the severity of them to begin with, so it would seem.

How could I now expect you to make me hear or believe that it is really over?

Or more realistically to even try.

I don't know if it's me or all men that have to be hit over the head many, many times, apparently before and after.

Maybe it is a caveman thing.

I thought I was listening then. Maybe I was.

I guess I just didn't hear you though. And I'm not sure what I'm hearing now? Even though I think I'm listening and maybe now you're not saying anything at all.

Are you?

Yes, I'm a man. I don't think like you. I don't feel like you.

I live with pressures I believe you don't even begin to understand or want to. Why would you? I don't know how to let down my guard. I'd love to.

That switch wasn't installed.

Would I prefer it different? Oh, yes. But I'm a man.

And I've probably hurt you in a dozen ways I didn't even know.

I surely didn't mean to.

Does it mean I didn't love you? Oh, I loved you. I still do.

But I'm a man. And the decades of voices central to my manly "domestication" left a lot out or built walls around societies' view of "manly."

I'm truly sorry.

I actually would have made my life a hell of a lot easier on myself and you believe me, if I only knew how. And it's probably safe to say your next man will be devoid of the many things we are devoid of. Hopefully for you, not in the areas I so lacked as to propel you into this wasteland.

But we're men. And it's not like we try to piss you off or hurt you.

We just don't get it, and that's something you just don't get.

It's not something we were taught.

On the contrary – it simply doesn't exist. We're men.

And there's simply nothing harder to be.

It's not an excuse, it's a reality - ours anyway.

Sucks, doesn't it?

So what!

I didn't cheat on you.

I didn't beat you.

I didn't fall out of love with you.

I did my best to provide for you.

Was I emotionally always there? No.

Was I uptight? Was I off track? Yes.

Did I push your buttons? Did I hurt the one I love?
Yes.
Would I do it again?
Probably.
But not to the extent of your breaking point, I would hope.
Did I learn? I think so.

So what! What was so bad?
And what do you think you're going to find?
So what did you really want? I still don't really know.
I know that angers you, truly, not my intent.

So what?

I'd really like to know.

A reflection – what do you see?

For over thousands of years, from kabala to Toltec wisdom, it is believed that all of the negative traits you see in others are merely a reflection of your own negative traits, projections and fears.

So what do you see?

And wouldn't that be ironic that if in reality you left me for the things you dislike or mistrust or fear in yourself?

Actually, that would explain a lot.

Like the victim – which you contend I believe I am, but I've never felt that way. That never made sense to me… until now.

And maybe I am part victim; you were always the victim in our marriage, in your reflection.

And in many ways, you still play the part.

What else do you see?

I was cheating on you, always. But yet I never did. Never!

Could it be your reflection or fear of cheating on me that convinced you so? And what else do you see in me that you dislike…maybe in you?

Look where it wound up.

No wonder this stuff's been around for thousands of years, kind of cool.

I know you'll disagree.

You always did when it didn't fit your reflection in the mirror of me…or you.

43 billion wise men versus you, man, do they have a lot to learn!

So what else do you think you see, or have you discarded this possibility too?

An argument…

Can be healthy.

Can be cathartic.

Can bring you closer.

Can clear the air.

Can get past the minutia, get to the feelings.

And is positively human.

But you don't know how to argue, or maybe you're just afraid to.

After all, it may not go your way – blowing up within minutes, spewing horrible things, always running away.

That's what an eight year old would do, maybe seven. Sound familiar?

You can't solve a thing that way, ever.

Would you teach that to our kids? It may be too late.

I can only hope they haven't learned it.

But even today you can't have an argument with me – that actually comes to a conclusion.

So how did you expect a marriage to work when you always cut off communication?

And why do you still do that? When there's nothing to fear anymore, right?

I know you think we argued all the time. But I don't think those were arguments. Those were your venting your frustration soliloquies. Your ears were never open only your mouth.

I don't believe that's an argument. Which might also explain why you never heard me.

And I'm sure you'll argue with that too.

Well, the way you argue.

I'm going to hurt you. It's inevitable, right?

You know sooner or later I will. You might as well get it over with now – no one likes to be blindsided.

Better to see it coming.

Better yet, why not control it?

Why not make it happen now, get it over with, move on.

After all, you're going to wind up hurt either way, right?

Maybe it was always like that for you.

Actually, there's comfort in the known.

Always happened before, therefore, it's got to happen again.

Better leave first, before I do, before I hurt you.

Oh, just one thing…I was never going to leave you, never entered my mind.

The other shoe.

We could hope that neither one of us would bring past relationship "baggage" to a new one. But the truth is that we all have "baggage" from every walk of our lives. From childhood to teen angst to adulthood, all our relationships to the present moment.

They're "voices" we don't know exist.

Yet we choose to follow their words, every minute, every day. And the scars, the wounds may fade – but you know they're there.

It's actually quite a miracle that almost any relationship has a chance of both matrices "fitting" to form one, true loving relationship.

And, we are always changing.

Therefore, the puzzle needs to continuously change and most of all, fit.

Are we all constantly and subconsciously waiting for the other shoe to drop?

I would submit we are.

Break-ups or loss are one of the hardest human events we have to face.

Do they ever really go away?

What do we know about past hurt?

Heaps…we never want to experience them again. That has to be such a driving force. I too have been waiting for the other shoe to drop – and why not – it always has.

Maybe I pushed its limits to see if this time I could be spared. But it's impossible to be spared if it's always another ongoing fear.

For we give in to fear and its power. And so if it's going to happen, better sooner than later.

If that same force controls your partner too, what chance do we have? We are driven to look for relationships that prove us right. That's just human. Or manufacture the situation to once again prove us right – like mistrust.

After all, we have to be right.

Either way, the other shoe has to drop. It always has.

And there it goes again. Maybe by finding, and by facing it, maybe, just maybe, next time we can keep both feet firmly on the ground and our shoes where they belong. But it's going to take a lot of really getting to know the shoe maker and to changing what he has always sewn.

And who is really happy anyway?

I'm sure they exist.

But I'll bet the scales of reality are tipped to the other side.

We live in a fast food society. We want it all now – instant gratification.

But what is it we really want?

We say a nice home, loving relationship, nice and safe children.

But why then can't we either obtain it or why is it never enough when we do? And what does that hold for our next relationship?

Is this just a merry-go-round?

Change your partner, doe-see-doe?

The scenario would tend to suggest that, once again, we need to change   ... ourselves.

And we certainly can't continue to depend on someone else for our own happiness. Yet, that's exactly what we do. So we spin the wheel, and hope that it lands on that oh so compatible person.

The one that's just right who finally comes with matching baggage, just a change of a new name tag.

But it seems that when we're ready to soar once again....we rush and grab the wrong bag.

After all, they all look alike.

As I said, we just continue to put different tags on them, so is it a wonder if anybody is really happy?

Or is it inevitable that what goes up...

The children. Remember them?

Remember the flightless joy when we found out?

The nervousness?

The anticipation?

Those births I'll never forget!

Simply one of the most amazing and love filled experiences –ever.

How can so much joy and love take a second seat to our shortcomings?

Why in the world wouldn't we fight with every last drop, every breath, every avenue possibly open to us to protect their home and sanctuary?

We didn't even give counseling a try – how wrong is that?

And what "voices," what direction have we now embedded in their faultless minds, in their purity.

Great role models, aren't we?

They wind up in a mish mash of relationships, step this, step that.

How about Wednesdays?

But I have plans this weekend.

They are like pawns on a checkerboard of visitations.

They live out of a suitcase kind of like hobos.

Oh, but they're resilient.

Really?

Shame on us, and our egos, they had no choice – we did.

These are our children. Don't do it to them.

I know you're lonely. I am too.

But don't do it to them so soon.

They need time to heal too.

They need time to adjust too.

I know you worry about your age, your looks. Society has seen to that.

And are you sure you've even healed?

Have you forgiven me yet?

So then don't do it to them… yet.

Don't confuse them.

Remember, don't make assumptions.

I know you're in a hurry, but is that really good for you too?

What's the harm in waiting? This is no longer about me or you. That window has come and gone; now it's about them.

We've taken away the unthinkable from them.

So give them time. Don't try and fill their wounds so soon, when you're really trying to fill your own. And if it's meant to be, it will be six months from now.

What can it hurt?

So please, don't do it to them, they had no choice in the matter.

Let them digest what they've been served.

Daddy's not coming home for any more dinners.

But it's still his place setting at heart to them…for now.

I'm wondering why it has to be all or nothing.

I mean, we can always make us nothing. So is there an in between?

Have you even considered that?

As we go on with this, my doubts increase too. Did you know that?

And maybe we just need or should consider a "time out"

It seems to work for the kids.

Is that something you would explore with me?

Should I even suggest it?

You can always get a divorce.

And maybe you're that sure it's what you want.

Therefore nothing remains for me to say or do.

So I guess what I'm saying is if you're not 100% sure, or even if you don't know if you're 100% sure.

Maybe a "time out" may help either way.

It seems to work for the kids.

And maybe at the very least we find out if absence does make the heart grow fonder.

Or, if out of sight is in fact, out of mind. I mean I've never known, have you?

Really, what's the harm?

I wonder if I can even propose this to you.

In your current state of mind that is.

Not that I really know what that state is, honestly. If I ask you to consider a trial separation will that somehow piss you off too? I know, what are my "ulterior" motives?

I say that because it appears anything I say or do pisses you off these days.

And I'm not saying that to piss you off either.

So how do I even attempt to reach you to even suggest it? The "time out" that is.

I don't know what the outcome will be either. What's the harm?

I may find that I like it apart from this craziness and you, too.

Does that scare you?

I mean, what if you wind up missing me?

Would that scare you? Does that scare you?

Maybe you are afraid of missing me.

But if that's the case, wouldn't it be better to find out during a "time out" rather then after an "all out" divorce?

Or, is all of this simply out of the question for you to begin with?

Would it seem like some form of, I don't know a retreat from whatever you're forging ahead on? Or has it even been given a moments courtesy in your mind?

What I do know is how much I don't know how to approach you on it, or on anything for that matter these days.

I am dammed if I do and likewise if I don't...about anything.

So now, I mostly don't.

Hey, maybe I'd wind up missing you more than I would hope or like to admit. And yes, that would only add to my current pain too.

So, I do understand if that's even a consideration by you for you.

Either way, maybe it's a gamble we are both afraid to bet on.

I hate this!

I really do.

I feel betrayed…by you.

Betrayed by what I deserved and the rights that I earned.

Betrayed by what I offered.

What the promise offered.

Life's tough enough.

Where's the sanctuary?

Where are the promises I relied upon?

Aren't I entitled to rely upon things too?

A natural order?

A Decency?

My own expectations?

An inherent compromise?

Of your promises?

Of your love?

Of a safety in our love?

A right, if you will, to be forgiven for my mistakes.

Or a lack of knowing or always doing the "right" things; whatever they may be according to you.

I provided. I took care. I was there. Always there!

But it was never enough or counted for anything in the end.

Your focus was elsewhere.

Everything taken for granted.

And that's simply not fair.

Not right.

Self centered.

So Selfish.

And it still is.

Just ask our kids.

You say you can't figure me out. You don't understand me. You don't know what's going on in my life.

Have you ever once stopped to think that maybe I don't know what's going on in my life? That maybe I don't understand me. That maybe I have come to a road in my own life that I can't figure out either.

Add to that my cluelessness about you, your life, and your motives. We are where we are, and where we're going doesn't appear it's going to be a fun trip.

You think this is all about you. And in fairness it may be about you in how you are reacting to me. Did you ever put you aside? Did you ever think that maybe I'm lost here too? That maybe this is where the "rubber meets the road" in a relationship?

Relationships are easy when they're easy.

But tell me anything that's easy in life. You're either friend or foe. You vowed to be my friend…didn't you? And forget the vow. How about integrity, history, need or just friendship?

Well maybe your friend here needs some friendly help? And maybe the help needed has nothing to do with you. And maybe your friend doesn't know what help is needed. What he does know is he doesn't need the added confusion, insecurity and pain.

What he does know is he could use that friend right about now.

He also doesn't know how to ask for that. Maybe he doesn't know he needs to. He doesn't know how not to be strong or at least appear to be. He also doesn't know how to council his friend, when he can't council himself.

You see the outer, have you tried to look past that to where it counts?

To the person you profess to know…inside?

Have you bothered to set yourself aside for ten minutes? One minute?

If my actions aren't of the person you profess to know, let alone love, could that maybe be a clue? Can you set yourself aside for that one minute and think… maybe he needs help?

Because… maybe I do.

You made your point.

I may not get it.
But, you made your point.

I didn't think it would be this hard.
Is it for you?
Man, I miss my family.

There had to be another way to make your point. No?
Even if I didn't get it, well, according to you.
Does your point still seem as clear or as desperate now?
Would your means to your point still be made the same way?
And I still truly don't know.
Is it a point?
Or points?

Where did you go? You were just here!
So where did you go? And how are you getting there?

Why did you go?
You know you really didn't have to.
Did you know that? Why did you think you did?

I know, you've probably told me a million times, but tell me again.
That pisses you off too – not my intent, never was.

I guess I'm just still not clear.
Actually, I'm even foggier now.

So just one last time for old times' sake…
Where did you go?
Why did you go?

Could you ever love me again? Or did I shoot that to hell too?

I was aiming for your head. I hit your heart, didn't I?

You knew those buttons too, didn't you?

I was really just defending myself. I knew your buttons.

That's how I was taught.

I think it goes back to the playground, actually. You know, guy ego thing.
Somebody hurts you, you hurt them back.

Kind of a learned reactionary thing.

They left out the part about when you love them.

You made it personal, or maybe I did.

But could you ever love me again?

I mean, if the button thing were gone? It's probably impossible.

I mean either one.

I've known it since the playground. Sorry about that.

I really was only aiming for your head. As I thought you were too.

I didn't mean for your heart to get in the way.

I didn't mean for mine too either.

You know we're taught to stand and fight for what we believe, what we believe in.

I believed in you...
Our covenants...
Our vows...
Our family...

But you're not programmed that way. Are you?
That actually would make some sense.

Avoid conflict. Abhor "violence." Just run. Give up.
Fight or flight I think it is.
Or are you just taught flight?

We really don't know from that. Not when it's critical.
That's not how we were programmed.
Right or wrong, we're taught to fight to survive as men.
When truly threatened.

If someone were trying to harm you or our family, would it not be expected of me to defend you or us? At all costs?
Would I not expect it of myself?

Well what do you think I was doing? Only what I've been taught.
Only this time, it was you who threatened our sanctity.
And most of all... our family.
Do you get that?
Or are you looking back too out of breath.

Oh, I know the "reasons" you gave me…

But when did you really go?

Were you really honest with me, or more importantly, with yourself?

When did you go?

Was there one specific time that you knew you would go? Did it ever subside, or was it the first crack in the dam?

Can you really say it was one particular incident, a combination?

And why didn't you tell me?

Did you?

Did I ignore it? Were you clear?

We don't always get it, but you know that, don't you?

Did it just become not worth fighting for, or did you even fight?

Frankly, I didn't notice when the real change occurred, did you?

Well, you must have.

I know things got worse but never insurmountable… I thought.

We're taught to fight. We're taught to negotiate.

We do it everyday and with people we don't even know.

Some we don't even like.

That I can do.

So, when did you really go?

I still have my gloves on!

And you've already left the ring.

Will you be my friend? Will you marry me?

I did ask you that didn't I?
I mean, I know I did, ask you to marry me that is.
It seems so long ago.

But did I ever ask you to be my friend?
Remember how happy, remember the excitement and trepidation.
It seems so long ago. Does it to you?

How in the hell do we go from that to this? How did we go from that to this?
Do you know?
But, did I ever ask you to be my friend? Were we ever friends?
I can't really remember anymore.

We must have been, or were we? Did we not take the time to build that bridge
and trust of friendship?
I mean, friends don't treat friends like we did and do...do they?

And when did we stop being friends? Or did we ever start?
We had to have been friends, right?
But friends wouldn't treat friends like this.

Don't friends listen? Don't they show compassion for each other? Don't they
trust in the other? Don't they go the extra mile for each other? Friends
certainly give friends the benefit of the doubt, don't they?

So when did we stop being friends? Or did we ever truly start?
Maybe that's it...
Because I just don't think friends treat friends like this, do they?

Maybe we can be friends – again, it supposedly starts that way, doesn't it?

I mean, we chose to be friends – at some point – didn't we? Or did we? Maybe we just took sex as friendship. Did we ever really decide we were friends? I don't remember talking about it, kind of just took it for granted. Maybe that's why we ended up taking each other for granted instead of taking each other as friends.

And now you're saying maybe we can be friends.

Isn't that how it should have started? I thought it started that way?

But maybe it didn't.

And if it didn't, how can we now maybe be friends?

Did we get that backwards?

That might explain a lot.

Here's the truth…

No, I don't think we can maybe be friends, not after all of that.

And if we never really started as friends, I can't see ending as friends or beginning as friends from an ending as mates.

I think we did get that backwards.

And that does explain a lot.

You know what really hurts? I just feel much betrayed by a friend.

You know the one I held hands with, the one I tried to comfort when she needed it.

Even the one I took for granted at times.

But my friend would understand that.

And, the pictures, what do we do with the pictures?

Yes I know I took most of them. No worries for you. I'm not in that many of them.

But my friend was…and still is.

I have lifelong friends from high school that I never shared what I shared with you. Yet, they're still my friends and always will be.

I'm just having a real hard time with that.

I may not even miss my wife at times.

But I'll always miss my friend…and do.

So how do you just stop a friendship with a bang of a gavel?

How?

Truth?

I can't!

So how the hell can you?

The hill.

Are you really better off now?

Are you?

Am I?

It's like the battle of battles, but we didn't take the hill.

You're just on the other side of it.

Funny, we used to try and take the hill together, fought the battle side by side, until we started shooting at each other.

Is it better on the other side of the hill now?

Seriously, knowing what you know, would you battle it again?

Or would you call a truce and negotiate?

Or even dare I say, communicate?

Would we both be willing to raise a white flag, knowing what we now know?

Or was it worth the battle?

Is it better on the other side of the hill now?

I know my kids scale it back and forth a few days a week, every week.

Do you think they're better off on both sides of the hill?

So would you fight it again?

Or is it as green on the other side as you had hoped?

I think of the holidays, family and friends over.

All of the hustle and bustle…The aromas.

Were mostly in separate parts of the house from each other.

But always a warm feeling… just knowing you were there.

And we were all family.

Want to know something else?

Knowing throughout the day – no matter what.

I'd wind up with you next to me before going to sleep.

Silly isn't it?

I actually drew strength from all of that… an inner warmth that I couldn't explain, or never told you, at least I don't think I did.

But one that was there.

Good or bad.

Secure warmth.

That's kind of "girlie" huh?

And I know how much I'll miss that.

Will you? Do you?

Would you even tell me if you did?

I did tell you, didn't I?

At least I showed you…didn't I?

Oh, and those holidays…

And there's always another one just around the corner…

For you too…

What are we all looking for, anyway? Really, what?

A better fit?

More excitement?

Does it exist? Is it better? Truly?

A bunch of walking wounded, from mommies to mummies.

Could it possibly be that you or I or both were just not happy with ourselves?

Can another really make us happy, if we're not happy with ourselves?

Did we bother to look in the right places? Like inside?

Would it all have happened?

Because I'm not sure what in the hell we are all looking for? Are you?

Did you find it? Really? Is it easier to look without me?

Or does it really matter, with or without me?

Do you even know what you're looking for? Or have you decided you know what you're not looking for, or do you? I can say the same, I think.

So why was I something you were looking for then, or was I? Were you?

And, not now?

If we were what we each were looking for, why are we now looking again? And what are we looking for? Are we looking for that which is not what we were looking for when we thought we had found it? And how can we be sure we won't make that mistake again? I'll bet we do.

So, we must not have really known what we were looking for back then. So how do we know we're not looking for it again? And how many hits or misses do we get?

I know once was enough. So I would submit that we really don't know what we are looking for if we thought we did then…. but didn't.

Kind of confusing to begin with.

So, what are you looking for?

Do you even know? Really?

Why do you think I had an affair?

I'll go to the grave denying it. Know why?

Because I didn't! Plain and simple.

So why would you prefer to believe I did?

That's what puzzles me.

Wouldn't there be more pain for you holding on to that belief?

And why in the world wouldn't it be easier on us both to give me the benefit of the doubt?

You never did, you know.

So why do you think I had an affair? I didn't.

But you choose to believe that. Why would you do that?

I mean, especially to yourself. There's got to be a lot of pain in that.

But there's also got to be some kind of perverse pleasure?

Is it self -fulfilling and is there more satisfaction in that self-fulfillment versus the pain?

I mean, it just seems that it would be easier to believe me.

I didn't have an affair.

So why in the world would you choose to believe I did?

I simply don't get that.

It must have been pretty bad for you.

I'm only guessing, because it also must have taken all the courage you had to break up our family.

Was it really that bad? That unfixable?

It must have been but I never looked at it that way.

From your eyes I guess I'm saying.

Truth be known, I never really thought you'd leave.

I just didn't think it was that bad... we've had fights before.

Maybe it was the sum of the total.

I admit I discounted your view because frankly, I didn't agree with it.

I still don't agree with it. But I didn't consider that it's your view.

And it must have been the truth to you.

So I guess it really was that bad...for you.

Was it?

Why didn't you help me help you help us?

We don't get it sometimes and maybe we never do.

We're men remember?

In our final attempt, you weren't really there were you? You made a comment to me; you said "I moved on before I moved out."

You did, didn't you?

So you had your mind made up even while we were trying to "fix" it.

But, you weren't really there, according to you.

So how could it have ever been fixed? You think that's fair?

To me?

To you?

To our family?

What was behind the scenes that supported you to not be really there?

Friends? A new romance? Fear?

Had to be something.

Did you ever think if we had taken a "time out" or counseling or even a romantic getaway, as silly as that may sound, maybe we could have fixed it? Maybe, but I forgot, you weren't really there.

So I guess I was just shadow boxing….huh?

Unfaithful? Let's discuss that.

You think I was unfaithful.

But, If I wasn't...weren't you?

I mean, If I wasn't, and I wasn't, then weren't you?

Weren't you unfaithful to me and to us by not believing me or giving me the benefit of the doubt?

Weren't you unfaithful to our covenant, our family and our friendship?

Define unfaithful.

Is it to have no faith in something...to not believe? You didn't believe me. You didn't believe in us. You had no faith...in me.

That's what you chose...you!

I believed in you.

I believed you would come to your senses.

I believed we could work through it.

By the way, a little hard to do by ones-self.

You were judge and jury.

Actually, you always were.

I had faith you would see.

I had faith in you!

You didn't bother to try.

I believed you would.

So, who was unfaithful...after all?

What did I tell you about him? You think he's your friend?

You think he really wants what's best for you?

He gets you all charged up. Ever stop to wonder why?

Oh, he understands and man is he going to help you!

Do you really believe he wants you to be divorced "as soon as possible"?

Do you really believe he'll still be around when we are?

Wake up!

Do you know what he does for a living? Really?

He fans the flames. The more we fight, the more money he makes.

Read that again.

He charges you up so he can charge you.

His job is not to bring this nightmare to a quick and easy end, on the contrary. Don't you get that?

We shared a life together yet we now have strangers picking it and us apart.

Don't you see that when this nightmare does end, he no longer gets paid?

So why in the world would he want a quick and easy end to our end?

He doesn't.

He's a lawyer!

He makes money on our continued misery.

Money which I worked so dam hard for.

Money that could be going to our kids' college funds instead of his.

I'd actually rather see you get it.

And when we are in his "web" they know exactly how to keep us there.

Don't we have enough to worry about?

And, the uglier he gets it, to continue his income stream, the more likely we will start to hate each other.

Actually, you can probably count on it!

That's not good for you, me and especially our kids.

Like it or not, we have to be in each others lives for a very long time. We need some form of civility if our kids are to stand a chance, but not if we hate each other.

Funny, we didn't need a lawyer to get married.

Yet, how clever of them to make sure we do when we are coming apart.

A time we are oh so vulnerable. It's the time of money, not love.

They haven't figured out how to get a piece of new love yet to fatten their bank accounts, probably only a matter of time.

They're in every other aspect of people's lives. Yet they create nothing themselves...nothing of value to society. No real business.

So now they live off of our pain and especially our confusion and anger.

And they fan the flames.

Why can't we just settle this ourselves? Why not? Can we at least try?

What's the harm?

Can you put your anger and confusion aside for one more hour?

How about if I pay you his hourly fee to do so?

I'd still rather you get it then Mr. Black.

Think about it. Think about it all. It's not their money, lives or pain.

It's all ours.

All our decisions... in the end.

How did it come to this?

That we can't even have a discussion for our own benefits and especially our children's? We use to discuss everything...remember?

Lets not do this, we've done enough.

Can we draw on something from the past...to try?

He's not your friend. I was.

Never forget that....especially now.

You don't know why I didn't understand.

It's not that I didn't understand it's that I did not see what you saw.

I did not feel what you felt.

Maybe I didn't try hard enough to do so.

But it's not what I know or knew how to do.

And so it added to your frustration with me. That I do know.

And therefore mine with yours.

And so around and around we went. It got uglier and we grew farther apart.

Our stances hardened. Our egos defended.

We lost sight of what it was all over to begin with… until it was all over.

We were at war!

And that became our focus.

To win…at all costs. But what did we win?

There was nothing to win there was only to lose…and we lost it all. Communication was now nasty. So around and around we went.

But where were we going? We were so very off course and one that we didn't even chose (if you think about it) maybe didn't know we were on it.

But now we had to stay the course for we cannot lose at all costs.

I really didn't understand from the beginning but now my egos engaged.

Maybe I could have tried harder but don't you understand I did not know I had to.

I simply didn't know how because I didn't understand and I simply didn't see.

What you saw, what you felt.

Can you understand that now? Can you try and see that now?

Would it have made a difference?

I now know that it probably would.

Couldn't you try and help your partner?

Couldn't you have at least thought about it instead of thinking about you?

Because this isn't just about you! This is about us.

This is about a commitment. This is about a life choice.

This is about a man's life a woman's life and a family.

This isn't a high school breakup. Those you get over. Or maybe you never did.

This is about an irreversible life change and decision.

Irreversible...look it up! You want to know what one big problem has been.

You have way too much time on your hands. You over think, you obsess and you create a world only known to you.

I don't have that luxury. I have to make a living each and every day.

I sometimes don't even get the opportunity to think outside of that realm.

You take that as indifference.

And you obsess.

And therefore you create a hole and it gets deeper and deeper.

Until it becomes your reality. One we all get swept up and under.

Like it or not.

Did you ever stop to think what if you were wrong?

Did you ever stop and try to help your partner or us? Did it ever occur to you? Did you lose all compassion?

Do you fantasize its all going to be different and wonderful? Have you really ever thought this through and I mean all the way through?

Have you ever thought that maybe you've created a mind's life that simply doesn't exist? But you always have to be right...Even when you're wrong.

Einstein said he looked at every problem from at least eight different directions. Have you even tried two?

Have you bothered to try and help? Or have you made up your mind even though your mind may have made it all up. At least to the degree you now wallow in and refuse to question.

And what gives you the right to not question or at the very least, not try and help?

Ever think there's something else maybe going on here?

Or have you even bothered to think?

I look around and I'm surrounded by a sea of divorcees.

It's unbelievable, actually. And maybe it's my imagination, but you all seem to be forty something. So what's that all about?

And why in the world would you all want to start over?

And at the ages that you are.

Here's the hard truth.

Men are going to look for younger.

You most likely won't be happy with older.

Older is very set in its ways. Older has more years of baggage too.

And older, most likely, doesn't want to have a ready made family or start another one.

Been there, done that.

And we're all divorced too.

So obviously, we didn't do something right in that past relationship either.

It's something like 85% or better of second marriages…don't work out. Yet you all rather play those odds, then the better odds you had.

At least the odds were more in your favor knowing what you know.

You already had a lot of bets in place. They say the odds are with the house. And we had a nice house too.

Now you're just rolling the dice. I don't get it.

I can't believe you do either.

Here's another little "odd" for your "end"… At your age, there are 8 women for every man.

And most of them you're not going to like.

If you are afraid of loneliness, you just stepped into odds that almost guarantee it.

I'd understand if you're being abused.

But sans that, why do most of you run so quickly when there's basically a wall waiting for you?

What are you looking for?

This is life.

Once around…and dam it, it's hard!

We are men.

Men do men stuff.

Different face, different personalities but we do men stuff. Get it?

Maybe you all need to take an inventory of yourselves before you change or try and change everyone and everything else.

But you!

You think you took the easy way out. It couldn't be farther from the truth.

You think we don't get it and maybe we don't?

But you're probably about to find out…neither do you!

Have a nice day…or should I make that life!

It's been a while now and it just seems so trivial, does it to you?

Or maybe sad is a better word.

I look around at some other relationships that have somehow withstood the test of time. Did you know they all had their almost "over"?

And actually most: many, many times.

What made them different? What made them survive?

And in their survival, they appear to have strengthened their bond, their families…each time.

Fear always plays some part in what we do.

Is it that your fear was stronger as to what would be should we have continued? Rather than your fear of what would be for you on the "outside."

Apparently so, you saw the path you took as the lesser of two evils.

But what does your fear tell you now? Would you do it again?

Sometimes it almost seems surreal. But it is always sad.

…And especially for our kids.

They were caught in something they had nothing to do with. Now they're caught in a life they had nothing to do with.

No say in either event.

They must take what we dealt them and they must adjust even if we can't.

That is so unfair.

What if your mommy or daddy had been taken from you? No say.

Can you even imagine it?

Aren't your fondest memories of your family: Your dinners, your trips, and your holidays?

And the safety you felt at night when you'd lay down and everyone was there. And they both tucked you in. Read to you.

Mine are.

We've taken that all away for memories of endless visitations, missing socks and sweaters and broken "goodnights" and I am sure thoughts of "what did I do wrong?"

You come at me in ways I've never seen.

And frankly, I don't have the answers.

I do seem to constantly anger you and I'll admit sometimes it is a goal.

But truth be known?

I think it's more that I just don't know what I'm supposed to do.

How I'm suppose to act.

You see, I've never been through this before and it's so foreign to me.

Don't you remember that I've never been that good at relationship stuff to begin with? And that was during better times.

Add to my lack of savoir-faire, the stress, the rage, the fights, the fear, the unknown. And, well, I'm sorry I just don't know what I'm supposed to do or how to act or how to....you fill in the blank because it's all a blank to me.

I'm a fish out of water here honey and yes, I know this part is all new to you too. But you are so much better than me at affairs of the heart.

You always were.

This isn't different to me; I'm on an even farther planet when it comes to all of this then usual. I hope you understand that or try.

Not that I expect you to... but it's my truth.

So know that I'm not trying to make things worse or to fuel the fire.

I just don't know how to put it out.

Or walk through the flames.

Which I do know adds to both our frustration.

But for what it's worth, I do hope we don't burn it all down.

For everyone's benefit.

And I'm not entirely sure I even know how not to do that.

You know who you don't trust? You!

You don't trust YOU to keep a relationship.

Wouldn't that explain a lot...huh?

When I speak of looking inside of you instead of constantly looking outside of me for something about me or what I am supposedly "doing" or not "doing", I'm not just talking about you in the here and now.

I am talking about all the experiences and wounds that are a critical part and parcel of who you are today.

I am talking about your dad, mom and all the relationships you suffered, you enjoyed and experienced.

I am talking about those parts of you and fears, you now chose to project upon me.

Think about that. And also think about this.

Let me help you. Let me help us.

And I admit, I'm not entirely sure how.

But I do know that I am so willing and in the remotest chance that I'm right or even somewhat right, what's the harm in letting me try?

What's the harm in you giving it a try...for you, if nothing else?

Because if there is a speck of truth to this, you will continue to repeat what will be a grand mistake, over and over again. And that just can't be fun.

And at some point, you will either have to fix it or reside yourself to a life of pain, mistrust and misery for you and those you profess to care about.

I'm here now and I'm so willing to take your hand and walk back together to walk forward together again, but this time, really together.

Please help me do that for not just us but for you.

I just don't know how to start.

I'm tired.

I'm tired of the attitude.

I'm tired of the indifference.

I'm tired of the craziness.

I'm tired of the anger.

I'm tired of the knot in my stomach.

I'm tired of the sleeplessness.

I'm tired of the fear.

I'm tired of that "holier than thou" thing of yours.

I'm tired of you thinking I know something that I don't.

I'm tired of second guessing.

I'm tired of you thinking that I think like you.

I'm tired of you thinking I should automatically know.

I'm tired of the faces.

I'm tired of you thinking you're doing nothing wrong.

I'm tired of you thinking everything's going to work out fine.

I'm tired of you thinking how resilient our children will be.

I'm tired of thinking about the missed holidays with my kids.

I'm tired of thinking about not seeing them get on a school bus.

I'm tired of the complaints.

I'm tired of the blame.

I'm tired of your selfishness.

I'm tired of your entitlement.

I'm tired of your lack of any gratitude, past or present.

I'm tired of this.

I'm tired of being tired.

And I'm growing so tired…

   …Of you!

The aftermath:

It's a sea of broken hearts, vaporized dreams, emotional walls and children's nightmares. And no one it seems will ever start anew with the excitement or openness of a young heart.

The bandaged, bloodied and scared meeting the other battle weary, trying to reconnect with a faded dream, a punctured optimism.

And if that rare connection should occur, it's simply a miracle at this point.

For we each walk on the mounds of shattered hearts, tattered memories, what ifs and so much to conquer.

The fear alone can freeze even the best of budding friendships…in better times. Yet we will continue to swim the moat and slay the dragons to reach the tower of love once again.

To swim up stream, yet we barely lifted a sword to defend what we once cherished and possessed; the armor of our egos weighing heavily upon us all.

Rather, we chose to slay each other.

And the lives of those we guarded…to do it all over again.

Even with the multitude of balls and chains starting from a cold and tear filled dungeon in which we've imprisoned our hearts and dreams.

We have no choice but to march on in the hopes that this time…

But what's really changed other than maybe a deepened fear?

What have we learned?

And what have we internalized to hopefully never cross this road again?

I don't know how we hope to find whatever it is we all seem to be searching for without looking in the mirror first and accepting both ourselves and the humanness of our companions.

And the children, what are we teaching them?

And why are we all continually looking for others to make us happy?

And why do we continue to do that?

It may appear harder to look at ourselves first, but in the long run, it's got to be easier.

How is it that we continue to lose that optimism, the joy, the attachment, the spark?

More importantly, how is it that we are all so quick to judge and to dismantle.

Why have we stopped communicating? Or why haven't we started at all costs?

Because the cost of not doing so is actually much greater then what we've been doing.

Why are we all so afraid? Why is it so out of control today? What changed?

Or were our parents just pretending? Maybe it's just not meant to be?

Then why do some persist and make it work? Maybe we are all too spoiled today. Life is so very fast today, we're so caught up.

And the grass appears so much greener... but is it really?

It's unfortunate the mountains we have to climb to find out.

As I stated at the beginning, you can always get a divorce. But you can't put Humpty Dumpty back together again as in the nursery rhyme.

Not for the kids anyway and not for the family.

And shame on us for not honoring our commitments. Or for at least silencing our egos long enough to truly try.

It's only then can you walk away, knowing and being free enough not to repeat this life altering mistake again.

And make no mistake; it is life altering, one way or another.

Instead of thinking it's easier to just walk away, even if it seems so at the time, try talking to each other for a change...really talk.

And try and understand each other and what maybe the real problems are.

And the best way to talk and understand is to simply listen...truly listen.

And try hard to remember that we are just men who can use all the help we can get!

And chances are we really do love you.

We are just afraid and can't admit that, we're just confused and can't admit that either.

And, we're just not wired like you. We just aren't.

Talk to us – we really want you to, we really do.

Make us listen. Make us understand.

And most of all know that you have to show us how.

"And in the end the love you take is equal to the love ...you make."

The Beatles

What is love? Probably top two of the all time questions.

But I think today the question should be" what is love...today"?

I'll bet it's different today then even twenty years ago. The "process" is probably the same, the "chemicals" the same, but the true meaning?

Does it even have true meaning anymore?

Everyone just seems so spoiled today, and looking for another to make them happy, so it too would seem.

And is it my imagination, or is everyone so damn scared today?

Fears of not keeping up, not getting ahead, not having, not doing, of emotion, of the past, of the future, of rejection, of missing something better...of life.

When does someone who professes to be in love, fight for that love?

When do they stop letting the past haunt their present and future?

Wouldn't it make sense that the past hurts were of a younger day, one that may not have even been capable of "love" the way it would manifest upon a more mature journey?

Yet its painful echoes reverberate well into our future lives and it would seem they may indeed rob us of what we so seek and profess to want to cherish.

But how is that possible to achieve if the waves that haunt and interfere were of a day when we were actually a different person.

And yet we continue to place our heads upon the sea shell... nowhere near our hearts.

When you're "in love," does that not bring certain rights but also certain expectations or ones' that a partner should be able to automatically count upon? Don't we owe each other certain decency?

An automatic moralistic and intrinsic code of behavior when one professes their love?

I'm not talking about not cheating, that should be a given in a relationship. I'm talking about defending and protecting your partner and that sanctuary, or what should be one, of love.

Or do we just throw the love handle about as easily as we handle other daily comings and goings?

Is love defined in the good times or the bad ones? Or is it a little of both?

It sure seems we all search so hard for love. But do we not give it up with one tenth the effort put into finding and nurturing it to begin with?

Love is a drug. It's a beautiful high. What connects that? What connects Us? Why one person over the other?

Does initial love make us look beyond character flaws or maybe not even see them, let alone show them to begin with? Is it natures' way of somehow making sure we get at least the chance to mate?

Why then would nature be so equally cruel as to allow the "drug" to wear off...ever? Would nature not in its wisdom try to insure that something fill its space when it does? Wouldn't nature want two people who truly fell in love, to stay in love and most of all, to stay together?

But we sure don't seem equipped to stay together today.

You can sleep with someone, share the most intimate intimacies. Yet, we can't seem to communicate with one another when things aren't going our way.

Was it always like that?

And "bad" or certainly, misunderstandings, are always going to happen.

It's simply human.

Aren't we entitled, when the drug wears off, to have it replaced by something much deeper, something much more real?

Something that two people can not only be able to say, but unsaid, truly feels as an unspoken love; a bond and a true soul melding experience.

Something you would fight for at all costs, for it would be equal to fighting for oneself.

Please don't tell me that is only in the movies. What the hell are we here for; to work away the majority of our lives, to buy bigger things?

I want to feel another's soul within me. But I also want to feel that I can count on another human being no matter what. I want to be defended as I would defend. I want my flaws to be a means of strengthening a human bond.

For that's what we are, human and very flawed.

And I want someone who loves me to love me with no boundaries as I would them. I want real meaning to those words of love. And, I want something far beyond words...

I want to always be given a benefit of a doubt no matter what.

And shame on me if I ever abused a trust so special.

But shame on you for doing the same; abusing a love, a connection that still to this day seems as close to a miracle as one could get. It is by all definitions….a gift and heaven sent and shame on us all for not communicating and causing undo pain and suffering in its place.

For who are we to judge another least we be judged.

Why is everybody seemingly running today? And where are we all going?

We must not be lucky enough to really experience love today. For who in their right mind would throw it away without seeking every possible answer or resolution first and foremost. But we don't. We throw it away.

And we do so every single day.

And off we go on our undying quest to find it once again when it was right here in the palm of our heart.

So is there really love today?

Or have our highs become too high to realize anymore?

When the pheromones shut off do we? Have we therefore come to mistaken the pheromone high as love? And when the beat of our hearts slows, do we mistake that for no longer being in love or that one is no longer in love with us? And is it then that we start to run fearing the fear of rejection?

Are we lost to making a deeper connection because we were mistaken in the initial connection as being what it should ultimately be?

Are we so blinded by instant gratification and surface today that we do not even know that there exists a deeper place for two people? We sure do not seem to know how to get there today. Or maybe it's that we just don't even know how to try. After all, we cast aside almost everything else today for something more gratifying or what we think is supposed to be more gratifying in something's place.

Isn't what we're all doing to each other and ourselves today in our spoiled and self indulgent lives, in reality, just more pain on our pain? And isn't the fear of that pain what drives us all to begin with?

We fight for nothing, even that which we profess to be so dear.

Where did we learn that? Better yet, how do we "UN-learn" that?

We're surface wimps and we pay a huge price for our lack of accepting our humanness' in each other, but mostly for not allowing ourselves to have a code of honor in our relationships. Whether a promise, an" I love you" or let alone 'til "death do us part," a little rough water and we set sail.

We are so quick to judge and pass sentence on each other and on our love and our supposed bond. What kind of bond could that be to begin with?

And why in the world would we not defend it and each other at all costs, to bond beyond belief; If we are truly in love.

We have to be missing so very much today.

Missing the essence of the true meaning of life and love, of breathing someone else's essence and soul; of a pride to be virtually given in effect, another's life, and then, an honor to be entrusted to take such good care of another precious life and to receive the same in return.

Instead, we actually let fear take over and therefore fear life and what it could all be.

And I'm going to bet that what it could be is what a loving God meant for us to have, to be.

But we no longer look in the well once we drink the surface water.

We simply look to dig another well.

So please do not ever tell me you love me unless you are willing to love me as I would love you.

To defend me at any time to anyone as you would defend yourself or as you would rightfully expect me to defend you; to believe me and in me without a moments hesitation if I have given you no cause not to, and, to use that belief as a basis and foundation when things get rough. To know there is always an explanation and only misunderstandings when it comes to our hearts and our love for one another.

To put the damn seashell down already for your arms and heart must be tired from holding onto that so long.

It's time to wave goodbye to the waves that have waved good bye and to always be fair to me and in return to yourself, to never fear my love or any communication between us.

To err is human and that's what we all are and it's beyond time to accept that in each other.

We are men who at many times simply do not get it, were not pretending, we just do not think the way you do but we do fear ,feel and hurt, the way you do.

Sometimes you don't get that.

As a man I can say without a shadow of a doubt, that my heart, once given, would never intentionally hurt yours and know that real love will make sure of that.

The only real sin is to not communicate with me and my heart when you say you love me, no matter what and to approach the tough times merely as a means to grow ever closer and closer in our love and in the melding of our souls.

To exhaust virtually every means possible to keep our vows, our promises and most of all our families intact.

Relationships are roller coaster rides and we all have to learn to take the dips with the heights and stop getting off the ride before it's time to depart.

Men do men things and the next one will too.

Know who and what we really are; we are bad communicators in relationships, we are taught not to show emotion, we are embedded with this heavy male ego.

We are men and we have so much going on, so much to take care of, So many battles to fight.

Those are not excuses. Nor is the fact that we truly just don't "get" things you suppose we do or should.

You know how when we're sick, you accuse us of becoming "little boys?" Here's a secret – we are little boys even when we're not sick .

We're just not "allowed" to show it.

We have communication skills primarily for business and for taking care of and protecting our family. We haven't quite developed the skills for taking care of your heart. Again, this isn't an excuse, rather, it's more of a plea for you to try and understand. Communicating with us may sometimes seem to you like pulling teeth. And, it probably is. But do you know there is a root there. However deeply buried, and one with deep feelings that hurt when exposed.

And with any initial exposure to pain, we instantly pull away, not realizing that once it's all out in the open, the pain usually subsides. It's really the fear of the deeper pain and the lack of experience or knowledge that makes us "shut our mouths", hide our feelings and retreat.

If you know the law of attraction, then you know your thoughts and feelings attract similar thoughts and feelings.

It would therefore make sense that during hard times, you communicate with each other not just outwardly, but inwardly making it imperative to hold good thoughts and feelings as hard as it may be to do during those times.

I'm afraid we just aren't taught to do that.

We spiral down in hard times and it's a downward trip that spins us both out of control.

So it's not only your actions, it's your thoughts and feelings which in turn can change both of our actions and maybe not in a direction we really deep down want to go.

I again submit that men are less equipped to shift their negative thoughts and actions (you hurt me, I hurt you) while women tend to hold on to the memory, action and emotion much longer, yet seem more equipped to "forgive and forget" easier.

Men are taught to defend our positions which, as we know, may not always be right.

Women hold on to the thought and emotion longer, but have an easier time turning it around and taking the "first step" if you will.

So maybe take that "first step" for us- no matter how many times it may take, until we either come around or you're absolutely sure you just cannot take another step toward us.

As hard as it may be, try reading much deeper into that which we may be showing you, for we may just be defending a position, and at all costs, rather than a true emotion.

It's what we know and have been taught.

We need to be reassured as much as you do. No matter how manly we may appear. For we all live in some form of fear of rejection. Yours just seems to be closer to the skin.

And although few will admit it, we really do need your help and know that we really do love you, well, the way we know how to love anyway.

The good news is we can get there.

But it would appear we have been losing each other before we do...

... or after "I do" anyway.

Paul Stanley Biography

Paul Stanley retired early as Founder of PS Promotions, Inc., located in Chicago, which he established in 1974. PS Promotions was the first agency of its kind and was ultimately built into one of the largest event, retail, and integrated marketing agencies in the country. He also managed new artists, the Great Ape record label, and was a concert promoter for 14 years, promoting over 2,000 concerts/events. He also founded the Royal Oak Music Theater and the Castle Farms outdoor venues.

Stanley created and executed the first corporate sponsorship of a music event marketing program. It was for the Ford Motor company. He created and pioneered the marketing concepts of Sponsownerships™ and Multiple Tiered Modular Programs ™. His clients include a multitude of Fortune 100 companies. Paul's "celebrity" marketing clients included a "who's who" from Sinatra, Bennett, Manilow, Beach Boys, to country music's biggest stars.

Paul has received many accolades during his career, but is proudest of being recognized by PROMO Magazine in its "100 Years of Promotions" issue that cited the six "main events" that pioneered and shaped the event marketing industry throughout history. The Macy's Day Parade and the Bud Bowl were the only two not created by Paul Stanley.

He authored the first book on event and retail marketing entitled "Event marketing; it's not about the Event!" He is currently authoring "The Redesign of Marketing and Sales" and is an adjunct professor on the subject at Northwestern University's IMC Graduate School.

Active in the community, Paul is passionate about keeping kids safe. He co-founded Kids Fighting Chance; a nonprofit organization that proactively educates children to rescue themselves from predators. (www.kidsfightingchance.com)

Personally, Stanley has 3 children, performs stand-up comedy as a hobby at major comedy clubs, is a playwright (his first play Klub Kokomo opened in Chicago to 3 ½ star reviews out of 4), author, musician, composer/producer, is on the Prevent Child Abuse America Blue Ribbon Committee and plays football and softball year round.

You may contact Paul at PaulStanley@MenGetDivorced.com

www.ingramcontent.com/pod-product-compliance
Lightning Source LLC
Chambersburg PA
CBHW031522270326
41930CB00006B/479

9 780615 164502